Original title:
The Parlor of Dreams

Copyright © 2025 Creative Arts Management OÜ
All rights reserved.

Author: Levi Montgomery
ISBN HARDBACK: 978-1-80587-131-6
ISBN PAPERBACK: 978-1-80587-601-4

Charms of the Everlasting Hour

In the clock's tick, time takes a dance,
Each second a chance for a silly prance.
A chicken in slippers, what a sight to see,
Sipping on cocoa, as happy as can be.

Lampshades are giggling, curtains hum tunes,
While teacups hold secrets of jovial loons.
The cat's wearing glasses, looking quite wise,
While socks form a band, much to our surprise.

Fables Resting Among Feathers

A storybook whispers, thick with delight,
Where penguins wear bowties and dance at night.
Chasing after rainbows, they trip and they fall,
While a turtle recites poetry over all.

Ducks in top hats strut with pride so bold,
As stories of mayhem and laughter unfold.
The night's filled with giggles from creatures unseen,
In the land where the feathers of whimsy convene.

Memories Wrapped in Dreamscapes

A landscape of pillows all fluffy and bright,
Where dreams wear pajamas and snuggle up tight.
A pancake parade rolls past on sweet trails,
While ice cream unicorns tell slapstick tales.

Balloons float by with giggles galore,
Whispers of mischief from behind every door.
When night falls it chuckles, a jovial tease,
As laughter spills out like the gentlest breeze.

A Haven of Untold Stories

Amidst the cushions, where quirks come alive,
Socks brew potions that shimmy and jive.
Monkeys in pajamas ride roller coasters,
While marshmallow clouds host the funniest roasters.

A ladder of giggles reaches up to the moon,
As jellybeans sing their own silly tune.
With pages that flutter like butterflies' wings,
This space grows a heart where laughter just sings.

Oaths Beneath the Silver Moon

Beneath a moon so bright and round,
We made our vows without a sound.
To dance with cats and sing with fish,
A quirky pact, our wildest wish.

The stars above began to giggle,
As we recited with a wiggle.
A solemn oath became a jest,
With laughter soaring, we were blessed.

The Rhapsody of Silent Wishes

In corners where the shadows play,
The wishes whisper night and day.
They plot and scheme, those sneaky dreams,
With ice cream rivers and chocolate streams.

A serenade of giggles sound,
As wishes twirl and dance around.
They swear to make the world a jest,
In their own way, they're truly blessed.

Charcoal Constellations of Thought

With crayons drawn on paper skies,
The thoughts took shape with silly ties.
A shooting star shaped like a shoe,
And planets singing, 'We love you!'

In charcoal clouds, we sketch our dreams,
As giggles float on pastel beams.
Imaginary friends in tow,
We sail on laughter's vibrant flow.

Strands of Fantasy Enfolded

In a realm where socks can talk,
And shoehorns lead a dance-filled walk.
With spaghetti vines and candy trees,
We frolic in the breezy tease.

Each fantasy a twisty play,
Where unicorns nap and roaches sway.
With every giggle, a tale unfolds,
Of wondrous worlds and laughter bold.

Embrace in the Matinee of Night

Under velvet skies, we sway and dance,
With hats too large, lost in a trance.
A moonbeam dips, it tickles our toes,
While giggles erupt as a humorist grows.

In shadows we twirl, mischief our guide,
Chasing our laughter, nowhere to hide.
Magic on napkins, we scribble our dreams,
With punchlines and chuckles, or so it seems.

Portraits of Enigmatic Souls

A canvas of quirks hangs on the wall,
Each character's smile spins tales to enthrall.
With one monocle, they stare with delight,
While dancing in socks, they embrace the night.

The jester's cap tiptoes near the wide door,
As shadows unfurl, we giggle and roar.
Each whisper a riddle, each glance a surprise,
Filled with the winks of comedic disguise.

The Cache of Forgotten Whispers

In boxes of secrets, we rummage around,
Searching for laughter, a treasure we've found.
Old postcards chuckle, their stories set free,
As echoes of folly return with glee.

A dusty old hat claims it once knew a king,
While socks tell the tale of a dance-off ring.
With each little trinket, absurdity grows,
And whimsy ignites in the softest of glows.

Silk and Satin Beneath Starlight

Under sequined robes, the mischief ignites,
As we waltz through the flowers on magical nights.
With giggles and twirls, we paint the scene,
And feathers fly high, like laughter, obscene.

The stars poke their heads, amused by the show,
As we whisper our dreams to the winds that flow.
In silk and in satin, the mischief prevails,
Crafting our stories with humorous tales.

Reflections on the Water's Edge

Bobbing ducks in a row, they waddle,
Saying 'quack' while they argue and squabble.
A fish swims by, with a wink and a grin,
Seems he's the ruler, with scales made of tin.

In this watery world, splashes reign supreme,
Funny faces reflected, it's all quite a dream.
The frogs lean back, sipping lily pad tea,
Chortling together, so merry and free.

Realms Untouched by Time

In a land where the clocks seem to giggle,
Time tick-tocks away, then starts to wiggle.
Sandcastles talk, with a wink and a nudge,
Claiming they're safe from the incoming flood.

The sun wears sunglasses, it's all quite absurd,
While shadows all dance, not a single bird.
Laughter rings out, in the breeze it does swirl,
As a cat made of gold starts to twirl and whirl.

Whispers of the Midnight Mat

A welcome rug serves tales it can't string,
Of socks that have vanished, and outfits in bling.
While mops and brooms plot a great escapade,
They dream of being heroes, through dirt they parade.

The moon leans in, just to hear every word,
As slippers debate if they're soft or absurd.
The mat chuckles softly, with wisdom it shares,
Of all the strange laughter that floats in the air.

Echoes in the Velvet Chamber

In corners where pillows conspire to scheme,
They whisper of laughter, and cool, creaky dreams.
Teddy bears grumble about missing their socks,
As they enjoy tea served on old shoeboxes.

Ladies in hats host a grand tea party,
Where biscuits are crumbs and the chatter gets hearty.
An echo resounds with a tickle and tease,
These echoes, they float on the soft evening breeze.

Chimeras in Twilight's Grasp

In the corner, a cat wears a hat,
Twirling and dancing, imagine that!
A fish in a bowl, he sings with glee,
While the lamp gives a wink, oh what a spree!

Couches whisper secrets of late-night snacks,
Chasing shadows, avoiding the cracks.
A clock strikes twelve with a giggly face,
Time is just silly, it quickens the pace!

A sock puppet argues with an old shoe,
Jokes flying high, like a wild kangaroo.
The curtains clap as the moon takes a bow,
Laughing at dreams, oh where are we now?

Tides of Ethereal Emotions

A duck in a bow tie rides on a wave,
Telling tales of excitement, so bold and brave.
The couch giggles softly, tickling your ear,
As jellybeans float, drawing close for a cheer!

Mismatched socks organize a parade,
Their leader a spoon, shiny and unafraid.
They dance to the rhythm of cookies that sing,
While pillows applaud with a feathery fling!

A star-shaped donut declares it a dream,
Painted with frosting, it sparkles and beams.
In this world of whimsy, laughter's the grace,
Where nothing is serious, it's all a fun chase!

A Symphony of Solitary Echoes

An owl wears glasses, reading the news,
While crickets compose in their fancy shoes.
A pair of old slippers debate who can leap,
In this quiet hall where silence can creep.

A lonely potato aims for a throne,
Next to a cabbage, both oddly grown.
They gossip of veggies, of secrets they share,
While the clock rolls its eyes, pretending to care!

A violin sighs, playing tunes for a broom,
As dust-makers dance in a soft, twinkling room.
With each note they giggle, creating a scene,
In a world all their own, where laughter reigns keen!

Gossamer Threads of Enchantment

A ghostly balloon floats high in the air,
Telling the stars, 'There's nothing to fear!'
While jellybeans bounce in a jubilant race,
Painting the nights with a sweet, vivid grace.

A sunflower spins, challenging the moon,
With petals that twirl, creating a tune.
As rainbows compete in a giggly contest,
The clouds cheer them on, who will be the best?

A sneaky old cat trips over a shoe,
And bursts into laughter, how silly, who knew?
In this space of dreams, where giggles unite,
Where whimsy and laughter take shimmering flight!

Echoing Footsteps of Yesteryear

In the hall where giggles swell,
Old shoes squeak, a tale to tell.
Whispers float like butterflies,
Nostalgia winks, and laughter flies.

Each memory's a funny clown,
Bouncing up, then tumbling down.
The past winks like a jester's hat,
In a dance with a plump old cat.

Lampshades sway with silly grace,
Shadow puppets in a race.
Footsteps stomp a silly beat,
While mice engage in rhythmic tweet.

Time plays tricks with its own tune,
Echoes of that raucous June.
Let's drink tea from a porcelain cup,
And toast to the memories we hiccup.

Mosaic of the Mind's Eye

Colors splash in dizzy whirls,
Thoughts like marbles, leap and twirl.
Dreams assemble with a wink,
As ideas hop, and giggle, think.

A patchwork quilt of silly schemes,
Sewed together from wild dreams.
Each fragment holds a jolly jest,
In a world that's never at rest.

Laughter bubbles like a stream,
Flowing through this vibrant theme.
Puzzles formed of chuckling arcs,
Minding gaps, and quirky marks.

Juggling memories, oh so bright,
Concrete shoes on candy flight.
Slip on thoughts like circus hats,
In this realm where humor chats.

Veils of Velvet Night

Under stars that wink with glee,
Frogs croak tunes, a quirky spree.
Moonlight drips like melting cheese,
As owls converse with giddy ease.

Night wraps like a cozy quilt,
In the dark, mischief is built.
Whispers flutter on playful wings,
While the mouse ballet softly sings.

Laughter bursts like popcorn popped,
Around the edges, jokes once dropped.
The clock seems caught in a spin,
Where every hour wears a grin.

In shadows where oddities creep,
Nighttime secrets make us leap.
Veils of laughter dance and sway,
In velvet hues that frolic and play.

Lost in the Labyrinth of Reveries

In a maze where giggles reign,
Every corner holds a gain.
Silly thoughts like rabbits peek,
Hiding truths that love to sneak.

Winding paths of whimsy greet,
With tickled feet and bouncing beat.
The walls adorned with jesters' cheer,
Whisper tales that we hold dear.

Laughter echoes, a friendly ghost,
Leading us where we laugh the most.
In a tangle of bright delight,
Chasing giggles into the night.

Round and round, no straight lines here,
Just playful spins that draw us near.
Lost in dreams that dance and cheer,
In this maze, there's naught to fear.

Enigmas in Clouded Reflections

In a mirror that giggles with glee,
Reflections dance silly, wild, and free.
The shadows pull pranks on the light,
Winking shyly, oh what a sight!

Jesters bow low as the fog swirls,
Spinning around with curls and twirls.
Each glance tells tales, amusing and bright,
As echoes of laughter take flight.

A teapot whistles a tune in jest,
Its spout a giggle, it knows no rest.
Cupcakes wearing hats, so absurdly grand,
Serve tea with sass, just as they planned.

Crackers chatter in the moon's soft beams,
Playing tag with all the night's dreams.
In this realm where the silly roam,
Each laugh makes the heart feel at home.

The Sanctuary of Cherished Hopes

Hope's a kite that can't stop soaring,
Dancing in joy, it's never boring.
With strings of giggles, it twists and turns,
While all around, the candlelight burns.

In this nook, wishes bubble and bounce,
Unicorns prance, and fairies flounce.
A teacup wears a grin just right,
Pouring sunshine to brighten the night.

Dust bunnies play hide and seek,
In corners where dreams giggle and squeak.
With every tick of the whimsical clock,
Tomorrow's laughter is ready to flock.

High above, a cloud makes a face,
Winking down from its fluffy place.
Here, every whimsy finds a home,
Where thoughts can frolic and freely roam.

Moods of the Fairy-tale Abode

Here, the floorboards sing all day,
Chirping songs in a merry way.
Each room is stuffed with petite delight,
Bouncing around in sheer, funny flight.

A dragon sneezes with a great big roar,
Sending slippers flying out the door.
The cats wear boots, the dogs wear ties,
It's a gala of giggles, oh what a surprise!

Mice in tuxedos dance on the table,
Creating chaos while they're quite able.
Each shadow misbehaves, oh what a thrill,
With every chuckle, they get their fill.

Walls are painted with tickles and glee,
Where laughter bursts forth like bubbles at sea.
In this place of nonsense, hearts ignite,
As happiness twirls into endless night.

In the Depths of Slumber's Embrace

In a world where dreams wear stripes and dots,
Sleepy bears waltz with pots and pots.
Knights ride pillows, on dragons of fluff,
While clouds giggle softly, 'That's quite enough!'

Pajamas pull pranks in twilight's glow,
Tickling toes, giving sleep a show.
Socks come alive, telling tales of yore,
As slumber croons sweetly, 'Just one more.'

Crickets play chess on a moonlit board,
Whispering secrets, never ignored.
In this bizarre, cozy slumber room,
Every snore blooms like a flower's bloom.

So close your eyes and join the spree,
Where nonsense reigns and hearts run free.
In dreams like these, just let it be,
For the funny whispers will set you free.

The Artistry of Lost Wishes

In the box where hopes reside,
Juggling wishes side by side.
A blender filled with glittering lies,
Whirring tales 'neath starry skies.

Socks and shoes, they dance around,
While cats in top hats prance unbound.
Pickle jars full of giggling glee,
Who knew lost dreams could taste like brie?

Forks and spoons in secret fights,
Trading tales of wild delights.
Each forgotten wish, a playful jest,
In this craft of folly, we're truly blessed.

Laughter bubbles from every seams,
As reality blends with our dreams.
Here's to wishes, both silly and bright,
In our realm of whimsy, there's no end in sight.

Gossamer Dreams Adrift

Floating wishes on a breeze,
Chasing giggles that aim to please.
Like jellybeans that dance and prance,
Wandering whims in a silly trance.

A bench built of marshmallow fluff,
Squeaky shoes proclaim, 'That's enough!'
Tickled by the tick-tock clock,
Time starts to laugh, a playful shock.

Butterflies in polka-dot suits,
Spinning tales in lilting flutes.
Candy clouds drift ever near,
Sweet sorrows shed a teasing tear.

In this theater of noodle dreams,
Giggles echo in silly schemes.
Adrift on whimsy's gentle stream,
Where humor reigns, like a bright moonbeam.

Soft Laughter in the Stillness

Whispers float on evening air,
Like feathered friends without a care.
A shy moon peeks through curtain folds,
Tickled by laughter yet untold.

Rocking chairs begin to sway,
To a tune that won't betray.
Smiling shadows share their jokes,
While sleepy cats can't stop their blokes.

Quiet giggles puff like steam,
From cozy corners where we dream.
Muffins sing a crumbly song,
As soft chuckles come along.

In warm stillness, wit takes flight,
On giddy wings, through starry night.
Pause and hear the humor near,
A gentle chuckle, crystal clear.

Whims of the Nightingale Call

A nightingale with a jesting gaze,
Sings of dreams in tangled ways.
With each note, a laugh ensues,
Sprinkling joy like morning dew.

A riddle wrapped in feathers bright,
Tickles hearts in the pale moonlight.
Wishes drawn in silly scrawls,
Dance along to evening calls.

In the garden, flowers grin,
While snails in tuxes start to spin.
With every chirp, the world's a stage,
Where mirth is found on every page.

So let the songbirds lead the night,
With whimsy, laughter takes its flight.
In this serenade of silly things,
The heart finds joy that laughter brings.

The Gallery of Lost Moments

In a room where laughter hides,
Socks mate with pillows in wild rides.
A clock spins backwards, time does a jig,
As jellybeans play leapfrog, oh so big.

A chair sings songs of a rubber duck,
While shadows dance in a game of luck.
A teacup tells tales of adventures grand,
Yet spills its secrets with every hand.

Naps become races on fluffy clouds,
And whispers of ketchup gather in crowds.
The ceiling reveals a tapestry of dreams,
Where giggles escape like glittering streams.

In this space where whimsy thrives,
Lost moments cheer, and fun survives.
A treasure chest of what we forgot,
Shining bright in the quirky spot.

Laughter in Bottled Stardust

Stars are caught in glass jars tight,
They giggle every time there's light.
Each bubble bounces a silly sound,
As dreams whirl and twirl all around.

Comets wear hats and dance on shelves,
While moonbeams tumble, wanting themselves.
A firefly chorus sings silly tunes,
Under the gaze of grinning moons.

Snickers pop like popcorn kernels,
With every giggle, the laughter swirls.
Fizzy waters tickle the throat,
While crazy thoughts drift on a boat.

In this bottled cosmic delight,
Laughter glows through the joyful night.
Unlock the lives of stars caught tight,
And watch the world burst into flight.

Diaries of the Heart's Whisper

A notebook spilled with doodles dear,
Ink spills laughs through every fear.
The heart giggles in scribbled lines,
As dreams leap forth from silly signs.

Puns and wishes glide on the page,
Chasing worries with a tiny rage.
Sticky notes dance in a gentle breeze,
Whispering secrets with playful tease.

The quill dips deep in honeyed thoughts,
While jesters plot in their fanciful spots.
Each entry a ticket to fun anew,
Where hearts can giggle, and the sky is blue.

In whispers soft, the laughter grows,
As pages turn, so the humor flows.
With every scribble, we find the spark,
In the quiet corners, we leave our mark.

Soft Crescendos of Dreamtalk

In the hush of night, where dreams abound,
Laughter tiptoes without a sound.
Clouds wear pajamas, cozy and bright,
While snickers light up the starlit night.

Pillow fights with giggling stars,
As wishes float on candy bars.
A serenade of quirky frets,
Sings to the moon in silly pets.

Hushed echoes join the frolic of glee,
As swirls of dream-talk set the glee free.
Socks pair up for a dreamy waltz,
Laughing at life's little faults.

Soft crescendos create a tune,
Mirth spills over like radish bloom.
In this realm where nonsense gleans,
We cradle our laughter, crafting scenes.

Threads of Fantasia Woven

In a room where socks can dance,
Even old hats take a chance.
Teacups giggle on the shelf,
Whispering tales of a jolly elf.

Pillows float like fluffy boats,
While curtains mimic silly goats.
Chairs swap stories, side by side,
Each cushion creaks with laughter wide.

A chandelier winks with a cheer,
Spilling sparkles, oh so dear.
The clock tickles with a rhyme,
Time flies when you're lost in mime.

And there amidst this jolly spree,
A rubber chicken sips sweet tea.
With every joke, the world's aglow,
In this place where whimsy flows.

The Sonata of Hidden Desires

In a corner, a cat plays piano,
With paws that dance like a wild soprano.
Toasters toast with funny beats,
While the fridge hums, and everyone eats.

A ceiling fan spins tales so grand,
Of dust bunnies frolicking, hand in hand.
The couch debates the best sitcom show,
While the lamp flickers, stealing the glow.

With sandwiches sharing a joke or two,
And a salad that claims it's feeling blue,
Naps slip softly on a warm afternoon,
As socks twirl to a honky-tonk tune.

Each giggle climbs to reach the sky,
In this symphony where laughs can fly.
With hidden tunes strumming the night,
Desires dance in a comical light.

Flickering Flames of Enchantment

A candle sways with a cheeky grin,
Casting shadows where giggles begin.
Its waxy beard flickers in delight,
As whispers of laughter fill the night.

Balloons drift up, plotting a prank,
While a broomstick lies in a drunken flank.
The fire crackles a raucous cheer,
Unraveling secrets for all to hear.

In the glow of this glowing glee,
A marshmallow sings in harmony.
With each s'more, a tale unfolds,
Of silly wizards and toothy trolls.

Thus alight in the warm embrace,
Humor dances in this special place.
With flames that chuckle and sparks that tease,
The night becomes a whimsical breeze.

Secrets in the Scented Air

In a room where scents collide,
Cinnamon winks, and cardamom hides.
Each whiff tells a tale so strange,
Of blueberry pies that dream of change.

Lavender giggles with minty grace,
As basil rolls in, taking up space.
The faucet hums a peachy tune,
While garlic dreams of a moonlit croon.

Each bottle whispers, secrets shared,
Spices dance, completely unprepared.
An apron twirls, sprinkles of fun,
In this kitchen, magic's begun.

So breathe in deep, let aromas play,
In the laughter of scents, we'll find our way.
For in this realm where flavors flare,
Life's simply sweeter in the scented air.

Soft Echoes of Forgotten Time

In a room where shadows play,
Old clocks tick in a silly way.
A cat in a hat begins to dance,
Chasing dust with a quirky prance.

The tales of socks that lost their pairs,
Echo laughter, light as air.
Whimsical whispers tease the night,
As tea cups giggle in delight.

A mirror winks with a silver grin,
Reflecting fables of where you've been.
A charm that sings with every sway,
Turns old stories into play.

So take a seat, let worries cease,
In this cozy realm, find your peace.
For the fun of yesteryears awaits,
Amidst soft echoes and playful fates.

The Lullaby of Slumbering Hearts

There's a song the pillows hum,
As sleepy stars begin to come.
Teddy bears wear pajamas tight,
Snoring softly through the night.

Under blankets, dreams collide,
With yo-yo birds that laugh and glide.
A fish in a bowler hat swims by,
Singing softly a lullaby.

The night is filled with cheerful quests,
Where every snore is a comical jest.
The moon does a jig, the stars all grin,
As dreams of giggles and fun begin.

So close your eyes, let laughter flow,
In the land where funny things grow.
For the hearts that slumber may just find,
Joyous whispers to ease their mind.

Wandering through the Gossamer Mist

In a veil of mist, where giggles hide,
Silly shadows move with pride.
A rabbit in boots hops by with flair,
Wiggling ears, without a care.

The whispers of dreams flutter and spin,
Chasing butterflies that always win.
A ladybug in glasses reads a book,
While silly trees with grins just look.

Marshmallow clouds float high in glee,
As ticklish winds dance through the trees.
Glittering secrets in every space,
Where laughter and joy pick up the pace.

So wander through this goofy haze,
Where every smile will amaze.
In this magical land, take your time,
To laugh and play, forever climb.

Encounters Beyond Waking Hours

In the twilight where dreams collide,
Whimsical creatures do abide.
A monkey juggles five bright moons,
While singing silly, catchy tunes.

A sock puppet waves, oh so spry,
With a wink and a grin, oh my oh my!
The clock strikes a lull, but who cares?
Time takes a nap under moonlit flares.

Frogs in tuxedos hop with grace,
While dancing flowers invite you to chase.
Giggles echo in the drinking stream,
As each moment feels like a dream.

So join the fun, without delay,
In this realm of jest, let's play.
For encounters here, we can't deny,
Are where our funniest dreams can fly.

Silken Breezes in the Night

In a room where shadows prance,
And giggles dance like socks on fire,
The cat wears a hat, it's quite a chance,
As the goldfish plays in a quagmire.

Up on the walls, the portraits grinned,
With mustached rabbits in a merry row,
Each wink and nod, as if they'd sinned,
In a world where they might steal the show.

Under the table, a mouse reigns king,
With a crown made of cheese, he takes a bow,
His subjects cheer, their voices sing,
As they sip mint tea from dainty cups now.

The clock ticks loudly, a giddy game,
As it declares the hour of glee,
"Who's next for fun?" it seems to proclaim,
In a whimsical space where we all agree.

Harmonies of Unseen Worlds

In a room where shadows dance bright,
Cats play chess in the dim moonlight.
Laughter spills from the cupboard door,
As spoons debate what they're meant for.

The piano sings with a squeaky chair,
And a sock puppet claims it's unfair.
Jellybeans giggle as they roll,
While a goldfish recites soliloquy whole.

Time skips ropes with a clumsy twist,
Tickles from memories that can't be missed.
The wallpaper whispers its ancient lore,
Of socks that wished to explore the floor.

Here, reality takes a backseat tour,
Where winks and nudges open every door.
The ethereal fret of a daydream scene,
Leaves the mundane feeling quite unseen.

Inkwells Overflowing with Hopes

Quills dance wildly on paper seas,
While a giraffe spills ink with sneezes,
Mice compose sonnets about their cheese,
And puddles reflect dreams with a tease.

The chairs are arguing who is best,
In debates about which is more blessed.
An octopus writes with finesse and flair,
While a distant fridge hums a ballad rare.

Pencils juggle thoughts in a maze,
As crayons fight over colors to praise.
With scribbles that flutter like butterflies,
Each stroke weaves laughter in funny ties.

Hopes soak the pages with playful glee,
As scribes live life as if it's free.
In this unique tale, nothing is stale,
Where dreams and giggles weave every detail.

Lanterns of the Unconscious

Lanterns swing on thoughts like swings,
As shadows juggle imaginary things.
Bubbles burst with giggles and sighs,
While the moon sneezes down from the skies.

A tap-dancing toaster steals the show,
While popcorn kernels begin to glow.
The secret of laughter spills from a nook,
As shadows play games in a picture book.

Dancing hats tip to the beat of whim,
While marshmallows swim in the ocean's brim.
The night wears stories of echoes and cheers,
As laughter blossoms, dismissing all fears.

In this realm, where smiles create light,
Even the grumpiest faeries take flight.
In the dance of the silly, we find our way,
To wake with chuckles each brightening day.

Gardens of Silent Longing

In a garden where wishes take root,
Sunflowers chatter about their commute.
Turtles debate under candy floss trees,
While peas in a pod hum melodies with ease.

A hammock sways, held by laughter's thread,
As whispers of pollen dance over the bed.
Each flower dreams of places afar,
While bumblebees tape a film in the jar.

With sugar-coated dreams weighing light,
A croissant tunes to the stars every night.
In this odd patch, where nonsense is norm,
The garden's delight breaks every form.

Seeking the joy in each silent plea,
Where the winks of the moon inspire the glee.
In the stillness, hope does quietly bloom,
Spreading warmth and silliness across the room.

A Hideaway of Unspoken Words

In a corner, whispers wriggle,
Chasing shadows with a giggle.
Thoughts bounce like balls in a park,
While socks dance wildly in the dark.

Jokes tickle noses, make them sneeze,
Laughter floats like a summer breeze.
Here, secrets wear colorful hats,
And every wall knows all the chats.

Dreams parade in mismatched shoes,
Spilling out what most won't use.
With silly hats and playful tunes,
Moonlight hums to sleepy loons.

So come and sit on the funny chair,
Where even whispers love to share.
In this nook, let worries slide,
For here, our laughter's bona fide.

Mirth in the Moonlit Hideout

Underneath the twinkling stars,
Laughter rides on passing cars.
Pinches of joy, a sprinkle of glow,
As shenanigans begin to flow.

Chairs giggle when you're not around,
And the lamp sings a silly sound.
With every tick of the goofy clock,
Even shadows play hopscotch on the dock.

Glitter falls like confetti rain,
Clowns juggle with glee and pain.
An owl takes a swipe at a pie,
While crickets practice their best sigh.

In this nook, the night's a jest,
Where laughter swells and finds its rest.
Join the fête of the moonlit bright,
And dance with joy till the dawn's first light.

Echoes of Lullabies Unconscious

Softly whispers drift like dreams,
Wrapped in silly, merry themes.
Ducks in pajamas croon at night,
While starlight tickles with delight.

Pillows giggle in their embrace,
As blankets smother with a trace.
Hiccups turn to symphonies sweet,
While teddy bears tap their furry feet.

Lullabies float on the breeze,
Cuddling with tiny knees.
Here, imagination runs amok,
Painting worlds with a little luck.

In reveries, the funny prevails,
Where each smile dares, and laughter sails.
Close your eyes, let joy ignite,
In echoes of the soft moonlight.

Flickers of Imagination's Kindness

A spark of whimsy in the air,
Socks tease each other without a care.
Giggles abound from hidden spots,
In corners where mischief's caught.

The clock's hands move with a wink,
While dreams paint pictures that make us think.
Kittens juggle, frogs can sing,
As we chat about the silliest thing.

Each flicker brightens up the gloom,
Like clothes dancing in a cozy room.
In laughter's arms, we skip and sway,
Turning dull to bright in every way.

So join this feast of the quirky night,
Where kindness wraps us in delight.
With every chuckle, the world's just fine,
As joy blooms bright on this silly vine.

Whispers in the Candlelight

In the dim light, hats dance and twirl,
A cat plays chess with a curious girl.
Giggles grow loud as secrets unfold,
The ghost tells jokes, oh so bold!

A frog in a suit pours tea on the floor,
He spills it himself, can't take it anymore.
Laughter erupts in this whimsical spot,
Who knew such mischief a match could have wrought?

The shadows eat cookies, they munch with glee,
While a bear sings tunes, oh what a spree!
Each whispered giggle an echoing cheer,
In this merry chaos, there's nothing to fear!

As candles drip wax like melting ice cream,
We float on our clouds, like we're lost in a dream.
In laughter-soaked moments, the night flies on by,
Till morning unfolds with a giggly sigh.

Tapestries of Midnight Fantasies

Threads of gold shimmer in midnight's embrace,
A llama in pajamas strikes a pose, what grace!
Juggling glow-worms, a sight to behold,
As the rabbit does ballet, so daring and bold.

Confetti falls lightly from the ceiling so high,
A squirrel in a tux takes a daring sky-high fly.
With each little giggle, the walls start to dance,
As clock hands tick backward in perfect romance.

A sleepy old owl recites silly rhymes,
While the shadows compete in elaborate mimes.
The moon sneezes glitter; oh, what a delight,
In a tapestry woven of laughter and light!

As midnight unfolds on this magical scene,
Each twinkling star knows what a joy it has seen.
When dreams blend with laughter, it's surely no jest,
In this tapestry, each night is a fest!

Echoes of Illusory Realms

In a world where shadows wear polka-dot hats,
A penguin performs with an orchestra of bats.
Bubblegum rain falls from sky-high balloons,
As the sun flips pancakes with magical tunes.

Chimneys giggle, their voices quite sweet,
As dancing marionettes tap their small feet.
In this fanciful realm, where waltzes are grand,
A spaghetti tree sprouts right here in the sand.

With laughter like music, the hours drift away,
Jellybeans grow wild, in colors that sway.
A jester spins tales, with his nose in a book,
While the stars come alive with their own quirky look.

As mirrors reflect all our wildest desires,
We blend into magic, in whimsical choirs.
Each echo of laughter, a sprinkle of cheer,
In these illusory realms, joy is always near!

Chasing Shadows of Reverie

Through giggly gardens, we leap and we bound,
With tulips that chatter, oh what a sound!
A kite made of cookies is soaring so high,
While socks with a purpose start learning to fly.

In the glow of the moon, the shadows grow tall,
Telling us stories, no matter how small.
An octopus chef is preparing a feast,
With dancing macaroni, the fun is unleashed!

Outlandish pie fights ensue with delight,
As the ant in a bow tie declares, "This is right!"
With laughter like whispers that tickle the night,
Chasing shadows of dreams makes everything bright.

We twirl with the breeze, in a frolicsome dance,
Each echo of chuckles a merry romance.
With every new twist, as we wander and roam,
In chasing these shadows, we're surely at home!

Shadows Dance in the Twilit Room

In a corner, a chair has a mind,
It giggles and talks, so unconfined.
Pirates pretend with an old paper hat,
While shadows conspire with a jazzy cat.

A lamp with a wig says it needs a break,
As a rubber chicken starts to quake.
The curtains are laughing at jokes unseen,
In this cozy lair where we reign as kings.

A dance-off erupts with a fluffy rug,
As creatures perform with a great big hug.
The clock strikes three, but who's keeping time?
In this playful haven, everything's prime.

A squirrel in a tutu claims the throne,
While a gnome sips tea all alone.
In twilight's embrace, the fun has just begun,
In a room full of laughter, we dance as one.

A Canvas of Yearning Looks

A painting of broccoli with legs so grand,
Dreams of a fruit bowl, a whimsical band.
Each glance a tickle, oh, what a sight,
As cabbage and corn dance in pure delight.

Brush strokes that giggle and smirk on the wall,
Graffiti of wishes that bounce and crawl.
An artist with pasta is crafting a scream,
In a world of odd tableaus, nothing's routine.

A canvas of longing, but in a funny guise,
A potato in glasses, its thoughtful eyes.
Each hue a chuckle, each line a cheer,
In visions of whimsy, joy draws near.

Paint spills like laughter, it's splattered and bright,
Creating a scene that feels just right.
In a gallery of grins, all just pretend,
Yearning for joy that will never end.

Crystals of Crystalized Reflections

Mirrors are giggling, they share silly sights,
As bubbles of laughter float into nights.
Each crystal reflecting the oddest of dreams,
In a world where nothing's quite what it seems.

A spoons-shaped specter is carving a smile,
While forks conduct concerts, all worth the while.
The glimmers are winking in playful delight,
As reflections dance wacky through starlit night.

A prism of nonsense, oh what a view,
Two toast slices argue, 'Who's buttered anew?'
With crystals that sparkle in hues made of fun,
In this fanciful realm, we're all number one.

As shadows are twirling, the laughter cascades,
Bright reflections join in as joy invades.
In this merry kaleidoscope, vibrant and clear,
With crystals of giggles that echo near.

Melodies of the Silent Heart

A tune played on spoons is enough to delight,
While a kitten in slippers takes dance flight.
Chickens in tuxedos tap on the floor,
Bringing smiles and laughter 'til we can't take more.

The silent heart beats with a rhythm absurd,
In a song full of quirks, we've finally heard.
As laughter takes shape, it rolls through the air,
With melodies swirling, who hasn't a care?

Each whisper a harmony, silly and sweet,
As cupcakes in chorus tap tiny feet.
The quietest giggles sing loud in the night,
In a symphony of joy, everything's right.

A concert of chuckles resounds through the space,
As the love for the funny creates a warm place.
In the symphony's embrace, we'll all play our part,
Celebrating the wonder of the silent heart.

Petals of Pensive Drifting

In a garden where socks like to dance,
A butterfly sneezes, what a chance!
With flowers that giggle, they sway and tease,
A bumblebee wearing a coat made of cheese.

A cat in a hat, oh what a sight,
Chasing its tail in a whimsical flight.
The daisies are chuckling, what a parade,
While laughter erupts from a winking jade.

A breeze whispers secrets, quite absurd,
As a fish recites lines, unheard, unheard!
The nightfall invites mischief and cheer,
Where tulips tell jokes that we all love to hear.

A snail on a skateboard rolls with glee,
As grasshoppers juggle their tea on a spree.
With petals all falling, a soft, quiet drum,
In a world where the wacky is never quite done.

Threads of Slumbering Visions

Under the blankets where giggles confide,
A dreamer finds marshmallows surfing the tide.
The pillows are chatting, a whimsical tune,
While stars wear pajamas, oh what a boon!

An octopus plays hopscotch on air,
With jellybeans bouncing, without a care.
The moon wears a crown made of sparkly fluff,
As laughter erupts, 'Oh, that's just enough!'

The teddy bears argue who's winning the race,
In a world made of candy, all smiles on their face.
A unicorn dances, wearing a tutu,
While rainbows are painting the skies that we view.

A sleepwalker balances cookies on toes,
While giraffes dip their necks in a fountain that glows.
In dreams that are silly, we float and we twirl,
Where giggles and laughter make magic unfurl.

Veils of Imagination's Embrace

A hat full of fish tosses confetti above,
While rubber ducks swim in a sea of pure love.
The crayons are plotting a colorful fight,
As scribbles escape into the soft night.

With lanterns of laughter, the shadows do play,
As whispers of dreams dance the worries away.
A porcupine tap dances on a soft cloud,
While rain pours giggles, bright, bold, and loud.

The chandeliers sparkle with glee in the dark,
As bananas and oranges join in their lark.
A circus of dreams, where the clowns shake a leg,
Where toast with a grin does a glorious keg.

The curtains are singing, a tune quite absurd,
While imaginations soar like a flight of a bird.
In the land of peculiar, each moment a thrill,
Where every odd corner holds laughter and will.

Dances with Phantoms of Fantasy

Ghosts wearing hats made of marshmallow fluff,
Spin twirling through shadows, who can get tough?
With giggles that echo in corners and bends,
A whimsical party where chaos ascends.

In the depths of the night, a raccoon plays chess,
Against a wise owl wearing spectacles, no less.
With crackles and snaps, the shadows all cheer,
For every odd pairing brings joy and good cheer.

A dragon in slippers discovers its plight,
While kittens make mischief, planning to bite.
With dreams woven softly in lullabies sweet,
The spirits pirouette on their ghostly little feet.

So come join the frolic, just follow the tune,
Where laughter is plenty beneath the bright moon.
In lands of peculiar, where silliness reigns,
We dance with our phantoms, shedding our chains.

Beneath a Canopy of Starlit Wishes

Under skies with winks and twinkles,
Socks speak secrets, tickle and crinkle.
A cat in a hat sings songs of the night,
While disco balls throw dreams, oh what a sight!

Laughter bounces off old wooden walls,
As teacups dance in whimsical halls.
A pudding jumps high on a jellybean floor,
Chasing the giggles that knock on the door.

Each wish spills like confetti in air,
As rubber duckies float without care.
The clock thinks it's time for a jitterbug show,
While dust bunnies leap, putting on quite a glow.

Oh, what absurdity in this bright, silly place,
Where dreams come to life in polka dot lace.
With laughter and whimsy, let worries take flight,
Beneath skies of wishes that twinkle with light.

Feathers of Forgotten Memories

In a land of lost socks and rumpled old hats,
Where giggles are whispered by wise old bats.
Forgotten feathers float light as a breeze,
Bringing back stories as sweet as you please.

A spoon plays the fiddle, a fork leads the dance,
While curious chairs give the walls a glance.
Lemonade fountains pour spritzers of cheer,
As marshmallow clouds fluff up without fear.

Old slippers converse with a wise silverfish,
Creating confusion, oh what a dish!
With whispers of memories tickling the air,
Each chuckle's a treasure, beyond compare.

In this wacky abode where the fancy birds sing,
Feathers tell tales that make the hearts swing.
Between giggles and hiccups, we dream and we sigh,
With laughter like bubbles, we reach for the sky.

Portraits of an Enchanted Mind

On the walls hang portraits with eyes full of glee,
Winking and nodding, they dance merrily.
With brushes that giggle and paints full of cheer,
These snapshots of nonsense draw everyone near.

A robot with glasses reads books upside down,
While fish in bow ties parade through the town.
Each canvas a puzzle, a riddle, a jest,
Inviting all wanderers, come take a rest.

With stories of penguins that bake cake in the rain,
And monkeys in suits who complain of the strain.
Every stroke tells a tale that tickles the spine,
In this gallery of giggles, all dreams entwine.

So grab a fine cookie that's shaped like a star,
Listen to whispers of where the smiles are.
In this enchanted realm, we'll laugh till we cry,
With portraits of whimsy that never say goodbye.

Mirrors Reflecting Secret Worlds

Glimmering mirrors with secrets to share,
Reflecting the sillies that float in the air.
A cat dressed in polka dots twirls with delight,
While crumpets gossip with a glow-bug at night.

Each glass holds a story, a giggle, a frown,
As shoes too big leap up and down.
With whispers of mischief that tickle the toes,
These mirrors of laughter, how everyone knows!

Through delightful reflections, a universe spins,
Where laughter's the currency and joy always wins.
With every bright shimmer, the fun never ends,
In a realm where the weird and the wacky are friends.

So grin at your shadow, give it a shout,
Join the parade of the joyful, the sprout!
For in every reflection, a smile we will see,
In these enchanting mirrors, forever we'll be.

Nightwatch of the Restless Spirits

In the night, they gather round,
Whispers echo, a silly sound.
Specters wearing mismatched socks,
Dancing here, hiding from the clocks.

A ghost in a hat, all out of tune,
Bootleggers laugh beneath the moon.
All the ghouls rock to their own beat,
While their shadows try to keep their feet.

One tells a joke of a cat and cheese,
As another attempts to float with ease.
Chains rattle, but they're full of cheer,
Turns out spirits love a good beer.

They toast to times when they were alive,
In a spectral review, they'll all thrive.
From the corner, a skeleton grins,
For mischief awaits, and the fun begins!

Paths of Golden Yearnings

Travelers tread on paths so bright,
With dreams playing hide and seek at night.
One hopes for riches, another for cake,
Stumbling on wishes that sparkle and shake.

A fairy offers advice with a grin,
"Try not to trip on your own twin!"
Laughter lingers in every step,
As golden roads twist, awake from their rep.

They meet a frog with a crown quite bold,
Who swaps tales for treasures not worth their gold.
"Oh, my dear," he croaks with delight,
"Don't trust a wish if it gives you a fright!"

At last, they find the place they sought,
But it's just a bar where laughter is bought.
A toast to folly, each raised their glass,
For richness is fleeting, but fun's built to last!

Reverie in the Enchanted Grove

In a grove where the oddball pixies play,
Mushrooms wiggle, dancing the night away.
They nibble on candy from rainbow trees,
While a squirrel juggles acorns with ease.

"An acorn a day keeps boredom at bay!"
Chirps a chipmunk, skipping on the hay.
While trees join in with a shuffling dance,
As starlight sprinkles a twinkly chance.

One pixie wears a flowered hat,
That made the forest critters laugh and chat.
"Why's he so silly?" a wise owl hoots,
"Because he believes in magic, that's truth!"

So merrily they twirl through the mist,
With reflections of smiles you don't want to miss.
In this grove where imagination thrives,
Silliness reigns while the enchantment vibes!

Dialogues with the Fabled Shadows

In the twilight, shadows gather near,
Chasing tales, oh so dear.
One claims to have met a dragon bold,
While another weaves tales from days of old.

"Your stories are shaky!" a shadow remarks,
"I skip around cities, ditto on parks!"
Their banter swirls in a comical dance,
As each shadow tries to out-romance.

A talkative figment boasts of delight,
Of tap-dancing under the soft moonlight.
"Tap on, my friend," comes a muffled reply,
"Just don't step on my toes, oh my, oh my!"

With every laugh, the world turns bright,
Where shadows indulge until the first light.
In whispers of humor, they'll always remain,
As fabled shadows weave joy from pain!

The Prism of Whispered Secrets

In a room where giggles grow,
A cat plays chess with an old crow.
They plot a scheme, a silly prank,
While sipping tea from a silver tank.

The walls are painted vibrant green,
Where alien plants dance, unforeseen.
A toaster raps, a fridge does ballet,
And every hour is a funky play.

A clock with hands that twist and twirl,
Calls out the day to a dizzy whirl.
The ceiling drips with laughter's hue,
Where socks exchange their tales askew.

In this space of giggling dreams,
Nothing is quite as it seems.
Each whisper shared, a tickled jest,
In this home of jesters, all feel blessed.

Breath of Enchantment in the Air

A frog conducts a merry band,
While fireflies light the night so grand.
The wind hums tunes of ancient lore,
As dragons play hopscotch on the floor.

Teacups spin with cakes that giggle,
Giving passersby a little wiggle.
The curtains sway with whispered glee,
As roses do the tango with a bee.

An elf sits knitting with a twist,
Creating dreams that can't be missed.
With every loop, a chuckle grows,
As marbles rain from friendly crows.

Bubbles float with jokes inside,
Each one bursting, laughter implied.
Magic fills the air so bright,
Where whimsy dances through the night.

Voyages Through Ethereal Landscapes

A ship of clouds sails on a stream,
With fish that jump and frogs that beam.
The waves are made of spun sugar,
Where silly octopuses do a flutter.

Mountains with faces grin and wink,
Caverns echo with laughter's clink.
The stars debate in a cosmic array,
While comets sing the night away.

A balloon with dreams floats on by,
Wearing a hat beneath the sky.
With every breeze, it tells a tale,
Of mice in suits who set sail.

Through wonderland, we prance and play,
With giggles twinkling like the day.
In lands where whimsy reigns supreme,
Every heart finds a playful dream.

Whispers Guided by the Moonlight

At night the owls begin to joke,
As rabbits in hats perform and stoke.
The moonlight chuckles, spills its beams,
Over fields where laughter gleams.

Bats in bowties sway to the beat,
While mice in slippers dance on their feet.
The breeze carries tales of delight,
Where shadows play games just out of sight.

A lantern goblin sings in rhyme,
Creating sweets that tell of time.
Each twinkle in the dark pulls a thread,
Of funny stories long since said.

The night is filled with sparkling jest,
As every creature takes a rest.
Guided by giggles, the moon moves on,
Painting magic until the dawn.

Shimmers of Starlit Reverie

In a room where whispers sway,
The moonlight dances, come what may.
Laughter bubbles, stars have winks,
While cats in hats share silly blinks.

Mice don tuxedos, just for fun,
Throwing cheese balls, one by one.
A giggling ghost pours in the cheer,
With a highly questionable beer.

Crickets chirp a clever tune,
As frogs wear crowns beneath the moon.
Wishing wells toss a silver coin,
And dreams take flight in clever join.

So sip your tea from cups of cloud,
Where silly dreams can dance aloud.
For every giggle hides a muse,
And makes the night a joyful ruse.

Lanterns in the Shade of Memory

In corners bright with glow of light,
Old tales unfold with pure delight.
Granny's socks, a quirky sight,
On the puppet stage, they take their flight.

A parrot dances, speaks in rhyme,
While clocks all laugh, they've lost their prime.
Socks and stories, nicked from lore,
Each memory a wild encore.

Balloons in hats, they float about,
Trading secrets, silly shouts.
Lemonade spills from the tree,
It tickles everyone, oh so free!

So grab a lantern, share a laugh,
Through the shadow, let memories quaff.
In the shade where echoes play,
Funny tales will always stay.

Reflections in the Gilded Glass

A mirror framed in laughter's grace,
Reflects the quirks of every face.
Bubbles float from lips of gold,
While stories spin and dreams unfold.

The cat in boots tells knock-knock jokes,
As silly hats engage with folks.
With winks and grins, the scene's a delight,
Where even shadows break into light.

Gilded fish in bowls of thought,
Swim in circles, laughter caught.
As laughter echoes, time must bend,
Each playful twist, a joyful friend.

So peer within that shiny pane,
To ponder joy, forget the pain.
For in this realm of playful glass,
Life is a show that cannot pass!

Chasing Shadows of the Mind

In a realm where thoughts collide,
Shadows chase, and giggles hide.
Thinking hats with wings and tails,
Race through puzzles, wacky trails.

An owl on roller-skates goes zoom,
While lampshades host a wishing room.
Bulletin boards of chuckles bloom,
As jester hats fill every room.

Silly whispers cast their nets,
Catching dreams as playtime pets.
In every nook, a chuckle grows,
Sprinkling joy where nonsense flows.

In chasing shadows, we might find,
The wacky treasures of the mind.
For fun awaits around each bend,
In laughter's wake, we'll chase, pretend.

The Language of Dusty Tomes

In corners where the shadows play,
A cat naps on a book today,
Each page a riddle, laughs awake,
Dusty words that giggle and quake.

A scholarly bat flutters near,
With spectacles perched, he acts sincere,
Reciting lines of archaic glee,
"Why did the ghost not flee?" he chuckles free.

The ink of quills begins to dance,
Each letter spins in a silly trance,
Librarians laugh with broomsticks tall,
While enchanted tomes create a ball.

With every turn, the tales conspire,
To spark a laugh and tickle the fire,
So come, dear friend, and take a look,
At the whimsy wedged in every book.

Mosaics of Serendipitous Thoughts

In a whimsical café where ideas collide,
Coffee beans chat, fueled with pride,
The sugar cubes dance in swirling glee,
Crafting sweet tales, just you wait and see.

Napkins sketch dreams of funny sights,
As cookies giggle with laughter bites,
A spoonful of chaos, a dash of cheer,
Creating mosaics as laughter draws near.

The barista juggles cups in jest,
While patrons toast to the silliest quest,
"Why did the donut marry the brew?"
It shrugs and smiles, "That's just what we do!"

Every sip spills secrets untold,
In this mosaic where magic unfolds,
Join the frolic that flavors the street,
Where thoughts waltz around on giggling feet.

Candlelit Serenades of the Soul

In a chamber lit by flickering flames,
Candles whisper secretive names,
A melody drips with honeyed delight,
As night shimmies in with quirky light.

The shadows hum a playful tune,
With the rhythm of the wary moon,
A light bulb sways to the beats of cheer,
While chairs join in, "We're all staying here!"

A matchstick springs to life with flair,
Twirling around without a care,
As waxy figures prance and twirl,
Creating a dance of dreams that swirl.

So raise a glass of laughter's glow,
Let whimsical vibes take you and flow,
In this funny serenade of the night,
Where every flicker reveals pure delight.

The Alchemy of Fanciful Whispers

In a lab where giggles blend and brew,
A fuzzy monster mixes up something new,
With beakers bubbling in jolly stirs,
As laughter forms into pocket-sized furs.

Cackling cats toss in some cheer,
A pinch of mischief, a sprinkle of fear,
"Why did the potion take too long?" they chime,
"Because it danced to the rhythm of rhyme!"

The cauldron glows with whimsical light,
Creating elixirs of dream and delight,
While hiccuping gnomes spill tales of the day,
As magic erupts in a bumpy ballet.

Each potion bubbles with joyous refrain,
Crafting chuckles from sunshine and rain,
So gather around, let wonder be found,
In the alchemy of dreams that astound.

The Quietude of Distant Echoes

In a nook where whispers play,
Laughter dances, bright and gay.
Socks are mismatched, hats askew,
Chasing shadows, just a few.

Ticklish thoughts that dart and dive,
A squirrel's chatter feels alive.
Teacups clink with silly glee,
Life's a jest, come laugh with me.

Floating past on clouds of cheer,
Silly secrets fill the air.
An echo giggles in return,
Each chuckle's twist, a new adjourn.

Between the cracks, a jest will bloom,
A riddle hums, dispelling gloom.
Join the fun, let spirits soar,
In this corner, laughter's lore.

Inside the Cloister of Illusions

A juggler's cat, a silk-worm chair,
Dancing socks glide through the air.
Pigs on bikes parade with flair,
Puppies sing, an odd affair.

Mirrors twist with giggles bright,
Wink at you in fleeting light.
Eggs tell jokes and flip about,
In this world, there's naught but clout.

Silly strings tie thoughts askew,
Crazy hats for me and you.
Fiddles play with playful minds,
In this space, oddity finds.

A peacock struts with grand display,
Bouncing balls that leap and sway.
Join the chaos, flip the norm,
In laughter's flow, we transform.

Time's Gala of Fancies

A clock that babbles, ticks in rhyme,
Socks dance freely, out of time.
Jellybeans make plans to fly,
Winking at the passerby.

The chairs pirouette with glee,
While hats engage in banter, see?
A rabbit brews a silly stew,
With giggles flavored just for you.

Balloons gossip about the moon,
Tickled by a pink raccoon.
Sundaes smile, winking wide,
Join the jubilee, come inside!

Tomorrow's peek will bring a jest,
In every heart, a merry fest.
With every tick, let laughter flow,
In this whirl, we dance and grow.

Journey Through the Clouded Veil

A fog of chuckles drifts and sways,
Punny ghosts in wavy plays.
Tea leaves giggle, twist and tease,
Drawn to whimsy with such ease.

Pillow fights with cotton foes,
Stories tickle as laughter grows.
Marshmallow skies and candy trees,
In this realm, we do as we please.

Hats that wobble, shoes that sing,
Journey forth, embrace the spring.
With each step, surprises bloom,
In a frolicsome, cheerful room.

Through the veil, mischief hides,
Come and see what joy abides.
In this frothy, giggling gale,
Find delight where dreams set sail.

Tapestry of Hopes and Memories

In a room where wishes dance and twirl,
A cat wears shades, oh what a whirl!
The chairs are giggling, curtains sway,
They whisper secrets of what to say.

A fish in a bowl plays poker for fun,
While teacups gossip, one by one.
The clock chimes awkwardly, lost in thought,
As spiders craft webs of laughter they've sought.

Balloons float high, they've formed a band,
Singing silly songs that tickle the land.
Their melodies drift with a cherry fizz,
Tickle your toes, oh what a whiz!

A rug with a smile invites you to sit,
While wizards do magic with a playful wit.
This space of delight, a curious zone,
Where every bright corner feels like home.

Murmurs from the Twilight Nook

In a nook where whispers stain the air,
A squirrel in glasses gives quite a scare!
He reads from a book of ancient cheese,
While shadows dance with giggles that tease.

A lamp with personality tells a fable,
Of a knight who rode a wobbly table.
The wallpaper chuckles, peeling with glee,
As a snail narrates tales of grandiosity.

The mirror reflects a clown with no frown,
Wearing shoes that flip up, twirling around.
It's a spectacle here, oh, what a sight,
As dusk tumbles in with laughter and light.

Tea leaves swim in whimsical dance,
As crickets join in with a daring prance.
The breath of the evening speaks in rhymes,
Wrapping smiles gently, as time climbs.

A Symphony of Timeless Fantasies

In a hall of echoes where giggles ring,
A walrus conducts with a feathered wing.
The floors hum softly, they shimmy and sway,
As furniture winks in a playful ballet.

Bubbles float lightly, each with a dream,
Of ice cream mountains and rivers of cream.
A mind-blown toaster pigeons coo,
While socks play chess with an owl sooo true.

The drapes flutter wildly, a breezy chase,
As mismatched shoes jive with exuberant grace.
A grand piano shares its secret tune,
Crafted from whispers of a silly moon.

The night wraps up all in sparkling jest,
Where laughter endures, a never-ending quest.
So grab a slice of this mirthful cake,
In this symphony of fun, have no mistake!

Ink and Petals on Fragile Pages

On pages where humor blossoms wide,
A pen does a jig, oh what a ride!
The ink spills laughter, as flowers bloom,
Creating a story that banishes gloom.

A butterfly editor with tiny glasses,
Rewrites the tales of past silly classes.
The petals argue with the ink's bold claim,
While mushrooms giggle and play the blame game.

The sun sneezes loudly, a glittering light,
As mushrooms ride turtles in a playful flight.
Each stanza bounces, tickling the air,
With rhymes that twirl like they haven't a care.

So dive into this carnival of glee,
Where every line chuckles with free spree.
These pages invite you with a nudge,
To join their merriment, there's no grudge!

www.ingramcontent.com/pod-product-compliance
Lightning Source LLC
Chambersburg PA
CBHW070007300426
43661CB00141B/304